Book 1

Python Crash Course

By: PG WIZARD BOOKS

Book 2

Hacking

By: PG WIZARD BOOKS

Book 1

Python Crash Course

By: PG WIZARD BOOKS

Step By Step Guide To Mastering Python Programming!

Python Crash Course: Step By Step Guide To Mastering Python
Programming!

Table of Contents

Introduction

Learning a programming language can be a daunting task for many, but the right guidance can be the differentiator and the ultimate deciding factor as to how well you learn the language. Python is an easy to learn, high-level language which supports both structured and object-oriented programming.

This book aims at making the basic fundamentals of the language clear to the programmers. The dynamics of the language have been explained so as to enable developers to learn fine coding skills. Python has readable codes and an easy syntax thus making it simple to learn. It has automatic memory management system along with a comprehensive library that allows the programmers to write programs in a fewer lines of code as compared to other programming languages like C++ and Java.

Learning Python can be your stepping stone in the field of programming since Python methodologies can be used in a broad range of applications.

Lastly, the book is useful both for beginners who want to master this language and the experienced programmers who wish to revisit the basics or want a manual for reference. We would like to thank you for downloading this book and we hope that the book is valuable for its readers.

Chapter 1: Preamble to Python

Python programming language was created by Guido Rossum in 1989. It is an object-oriented, multi-purpose and interactive scripting language. The language has been designed as highly readable. Python has fewer syntactical constructions and uses English keywords frequently. It is considered as a great language for beginners in the programming field.

Features of Python

1. Python provides rich data types and easier to read syntax as compared to other languages.
2. As compared to other programming languages it allows more run-time flexibility.
3. It is a platform independent scripted language with complete access to operating system API's.
4. Python libraries are cross-platform, thus making them compatible with Windows, MacIntosh and Linux.
5. It supports interactive mode that allows snippets of codes to be tested and debugged interactively.
6. It is a portable language and can run of various hardware platforms with same interface.
7. The Python source code can be easily maintained.
8. It provides support and an enhanced structure for big programs than shell scripting.
9. For building large applications, python can be assembled in to byte-code.
10. Python can be effortlessly incorporated with JAVA , C++, C , COBRA and Active X.
11. It can be used for programming video games, various scientific programs and artificial intelligence algorithms.
12. It has automatic memory management system.

Python is a self-sufficient language and consists of many tools and once the programmer becomes aware of their uses then it becomes an easy task for them. The language makes a solid foundation to branch out and learn other programming languages.

Python Crash Course: Step By Step Guide To Mastering Python Programming!

Installing and Setting Up Python

Python distribution is available for wide range of platforms. It is easy to install and nowadays many Linux and Unix distributions include the latest version of Python. To download and install Python you can visit http://www.python.org/downloads/ and opt for the desired version. Even though version 3 is the latest but still Python 2 is used widely. Once you have downloaded and installed you need to set up the path. To add the Python directory for a particular session in-

Linux /UNIX –

a) In the csh shell type setenv PATH "$PATH:/usr/local/bin/python" then press Enter.
b) For Linux, in the bash shell, type export ATH= "$PATH:/usr/local/bin/Python" then press Enter.
c) Type PATH="$PATH:/usr/local/bin/Python" in the sh or ksh shell and press Enter.
d) Please note that /usr/local/bin/Python is the path of the Python directory.

Windows-

a) Type path %path%;C:\Python at the command prompt and press Enter.
b) The path of Python directory is C:\Python

Running Python

There are three different ways to start Python. Python can be started from DOS, UNIX or any other system that gives you a shell window or a command-line interpreter. You can right away start coding in the interactive interpreter-

```
C: > python #Windows/ DOS
Or
python% #Unix/Linux
or
$python #Unix/Linux
```

A python script can be executed at command line by invoking the interpreter on your application.

IDE – Integrated Development Environment

You can run Python from GUI (Graphical User Interface) environment as well, provided you have a GUI application on your system that supports Python.

1. IDLE is the very first Unix IDE for Python.
2. For Python, PythonWin is the first Windows interface and is an IDE with a GUI.
3. From the main website the Macintosh version of python along with IDLE and IDE can be downloaded either as BinHex's files or MacBinary.

Make sure the Python environment is set up properly and is working fine so that you can execute your codes easily. (Python - Environment Setup)

Chapter 2: Basic Syntax

In the previous chapter, we learned how to install and set up Python. This chapter we will discuss the Python Syntax. A set of rules that defines how a program will be written and interpreted is called Syntax.

Let's understand various methods of programming

Interactive Mode Programming

At the command prompt type the below mentioned text and press Enter

print "Hello, Python!"

The output in version 2.4.3 will be *Hello,Python!*. Incase you are using the new version then you will have to use parenthesis along with the print statement–

print ("Goodmorning, Python!");

Script mode programming

The execution of script begins and continues till the script the finished upon invoking the interpreter with script parameter. As soon as the script finishes the interpreter will not be active any more. To understand it better take a look at this simple program.

Python files have extension **.py.** Type the source code *print "Hello, Python!"* in a test.pyf file and try to run the program as - *$ python test.py*. It will generate the following output –

Hello, Python!

Now presuming the availability of Python interpreter in /usr/bin directory, run
the program as-

$ chmod +x test.py   # to make the file executable

$ ./test.py

Output will be –

Hello, Python!

Identifies in Python

A name which is used to recognize a variable, class, function, module or other
subject in Python is called as an identifier. An identifier begins with a to z or A to
Z letters or a _ (underscore) which is followed more letters or a zero, digits (0 to
9) and underscores. No punctuation characters like %, $, @ are allowed within
Python identifiers. It is a case dependent language.

a) Class names begin with uppercase letters and all other identifiers begin
   with a lowercase letter.
b) An identifier which begins with a single foremost underscore indicates that
   it is private.
c) An identifier with two leading underscore denotes a strongly private
   identifier.
d) The identifier is a language-defined special name in case it ends with two
   trailing underscores.

Reserved Words

There are certain reserved words in Python which cannot be used as variable or a
constant or any other identifier name. All reserved words are in lowercase only.

not	exec	and
or	finally	assert
pass	for	break
print	from	class
raise	global	continue
return	if	def
try	import	del
while	in	elif
with	is	else
yield	lambda	except

Lines and Indentation

In Python, to indicate blocks of code for function and class definitions or flow control, there are no braces. The line indentation denotes the block of codes. In the indentation, the number of spaces is variable, but inside the block same amount of indentation should be done for all statements. Therefore, a block is formed by all the unbroken lines which have been indented with same number of spaces.

Multi-Line Statements

A new line in Python typically marks the end of a statement. However, the use of line continuation character (\) is allowed to denote the line should continue. Example –

```
Total = goods_one + \
    goods_two + \
    goods_three + \
```

The line continuation character is not required for statements contained within brackets ( ), [ ] or { }.

Python Crash Course: Step By Step Guide To Mastering Python Programming!

Quotation

In python, all three quotes (' , " or """) are accepted. These indicate string literals provided the same kind of quote begins and closes the string. To cover the string across multiple lines, triple quotes are used.

Comments

The comment in Python begins with a hash (#) sign that is not within the string literal. After the hash all characters up to the end of the physical line form a part of the comment. However, they are ignored by the Python interpreter.

Blank lines

Blank lines are ignored by Python. These are the lines which have just whitespace, probably with a comment.

Multiple Statements on a Single line

On a single line multiple statements are allowed with a semicolon (;) provided that none of the statement starts a new code block.

Suites

In Python, a single code of block made by a cluster of statements is called as suites. The compound statements like if, else, while, def and class need a suite and a header line. The header lines start with statement (including keyword) and a colon denotes the end. They are trailed by one or more lines that make a suite.

Chapter 3: Python Fundamentals

Now that we know the syntax of Python, it is imperative for programmers to understand the python fundamentals. In other words, we would be discussing the basics on which the Python programming is based.

VARIABLES

A reserved memory location where values are stored is known as a variable. Memory space is allocated by the python interpreter and on the basis of data type of a variable it takes decision on what to store in this reserved memory. Hence, in the variables storing of characters, integers, or decimals is possible by assigning them different data types.

<u>How to assign values to variables?</u>

For assigning values to the variables you need to use the equal (=) sign. The left hand side operand denotes the variable name and the right side operand denotes the stored value inside the variable. Example –

```
counter = 10                        (integer assignment)
miles   = 100                         (floating point)
name   = "Tom"                    (string)

print counter
print miles
print names
```

In the above example-10, 100 and Tom are the values assigned to counter, miles and name variables respectively and will give us the result as –
10
100
Tom

Assigning a lone value to numerous variables at the same time is also possible.

Example –
x= y= z= 1

In the above example, with value 1, the integer object is created, and same memory location is assigned to all three variables. Apart from this multiple objects can also be assigned to several variables. Like –
x, y, z = 1, 2, "Tom"

Data types

There are many types of data which are reserved in memory such as; age of a person is defined in numbers, and his address is defined as alphanumeric. To define the operations possible there are several standard data types which are used. We are just writing a brief on them as of now and these will be explained in detail in next chapters .They are –

a) Numbers – As the name suggests numeric values are stored in this data type. Upon assigning a value to them number objects are created. Various numerical types that supported by Python are–
(1) Signed integers (int) e.g. – 2, 4, 44 etc.
(2) Long integers (long), they can be depicted in hexadecimal and octal as well. e.g.- 0122L, -0x19323L etc.
(3) Floating point real values (float) e.g. – 5.0, 2.22, -88.88 etc.
(4) Complex numbers (complex) e.g. – 3e+26j, 45.j etc.

b) Strings –The adjoining set of characters depicted in quotation marks are called strings. Both single and double quotes are allowed in Python. The concatenation operator is represented as plus sign (+) and the repetition operator is represented as (*) asterisk.

c) Lists – These are mainly flexible data types in Python. The items in a list are separated by a comma and are written inside square brackets. The concatenation operator is represented as plus sign (+) and the repetition operator is represented as (*) asterisk.

d) Tuples - It is data type in sequence, similar to lists. A comma separates the number of values contained in tuples and unlike lists they are enclosed in parenthesis. Lists cannot be updated.

e) Dictionary – Dictionaries in Python are hash table types. They function like hashes or associative arrays and consist of key-value pairs. The dictionary keys are typically numbers or strings. The curly braces enclose the dictionaries and by using ([ ]) square brackets values can be accessed and assigned. For example, to create, add and delete entries in dictionary

```
# make a phone book:
phonebook = {'Tom Halter': 665544, \
'Liza Raymond': 889966, 'Ronald Johnson': 776655, \
'Kim Lee': 443344}

# add the person 'Mathew Peterson' to the phonebook:
phonebook ['Mathew Peterson'] = 99887766

del phonebook ['Kim Lee']
```

OPERATORS

The constructs which can manipulate the value of an operand are known as operators.

Python operators

1. **Arithmetic**

   These operators execute various arithmetic calculations like addition, subtraction, division, multiplication, exponent, %modulus etc. For arithmetic calculation, there are various methods in Python like you can use the eval function, calculate and declare variable, or call functions.
   Let us take a simple example –
   ```
   a = 4
   b = 5
   print a + b
   ```

   Output will be "9". Similarly other arithmetic operators like division (/), multiplication (*), exponent (**) etc. can be used.

2. **Comparison**

   The comparison operator compares the value on either side of the operand to determine the relation between them. Various comparison operators are (!=, ==, >, <, <=, >=).

Example – we will compare the value of a to the value of b and print the result in true or false. Assume value of a =4 which is smaller than b =5. Now when we print the value as a >b, it actually compares the value of a to b and since it is incorrect, it returns as false. Similarly you can use other comparison operators.

3. Assignment

To assign the value of the right operand to the left operand, we use assignment operators.They are (+, +=, -=, /=, *=, %=, **=, //=). Example-

num1 = 4
num2 =5
print ("Line1 – Value of num1:" , num1)
print ("Line2 – Value of num2:", num2)

Output –

('Line1 –Value of num1:',4)
('Line2 – value of num2:', 5

4. Logical

These operators are used for conditional statements which are true or false.
AND, OR and NOT are the logical operators in Python
AND – it returns TRUE if both left and right operands are true.
OR – it returns FALSE if either of the operand is true.
NOT – it returns TRUE if operand is false

Example-
x = true
y = false
print ('x and y is', x and y)
print ('x or y is', x or y)
print ('not x is', not x)

The result will be –
('x and y is', False)

('x or y is', True)
('not x is', False)

5. Membership

Inside a sequence such as strings, lists or tuples membership is checked by these operators. These are of two types (in and not in). These operators give result based on the variable present in specified string or sequence.
Example –
We will check whether value of x=3 and y=7 is available in list or not by using membership operators.

x= 3
y =7
list = [1, 2, 3, 4, 5];

if (x in list):
    print "Line 1 – x is available in the given list"
else:
     print "Line 1 – x is not available in the given list"

if (y not in list):
    print "Line 2 – y is not available in the given list"
else:
     print "Line 2- y is available in the given list"

Result of the above code –

Line 1 – x is available in the given list
Line 2 – y is not available in the given list

6. Identity

Memory locations of two objects are compared by identity operators. They are of two types – is and is not.
is – it returns true if two variables point the same object otherwise false.
is not- it returns false if two variables point the same object, otherwise true.

Example –

x = 10

y = 10

if (x is y):

    print "x & y SAME identity"

y = 20

if (x is not y):

    print "x & y have DIFFERENT identity"

Following result is generated –
x&y SAME identity
x & y DIFFERENT identity

7. **Bitwise**

A bitwise operator work on bits and performs bit by bit operation. Python supports the following Bitwise operators - & Binary AND, | Binary OR, ^ Binary XOR, ~Binary Ones Complement, << Binary Left shift and >> Binary Right shift.

Operators Precedence

It determines which operator needs to be evaluated first. Precedence of operators is necessary to avoid ambiguity in values. For example – multiplication has a higher precedence than addition. Following operators are usedin Python – (**, ~+ -, */ % //, + -, & , ^|, >><<, &, <=<>>=, <> == !=, is is not, in not in , not or and)

STATEMENTS

Anticipating the conditions that might occur while executing a program and specifying the actions according to those conditions is called decision making. The decision structures assess numerous expressions which produce TRUE or FALSE as a result. You need to determine which action to take and what statements to execute if the result is TRUE or FALSE otherwise. In Python programming any non-zero and non-null values are assumed as TRUE, and if it is either null or zero then it is assumed as FALSE value.

Following types of decision making statements are provided in Python –

1. **if statements** - it contains a Boolean expression followed by one or more statements.

   A logical expression is used to compare the data and decision is made on the basis of comparison result. If Boolean expression evaluates to TRUE, then the block of statement(s) inside the *if* statement is executed. In case it evaluates FALSE, then the first set of code after the end of *if* statement is executed.

   Syntax –
   if expression:
   * statement(s)*

2. **if....else statements** – In this an *if* statement is followed by an optional *else* statement.If the conditional expression in the *if* statement resolves to FALSE value or 0, the block of code executes in an else statement.

   Syntax –
   if expression:
   * statement(s)*
   else:
   * statement(s)*

3. **elif statement** – It permits you to examine multiple expressions for TRUE and carry out a block of code as soon as one of the condition evaluates to TRUE. They are also optional statements and random number of *elif* statements following an *if* can be there.

   Syntax –
   if expression 1:
   * statement(s)*
   if expression 2:
   * statement(s)*
   elif expression3:
   * statement(s)*
   else:

statement(s)

4. **nested statements** – When you want to examine a different condition when a condition works out to be true then you can use *nested if* statements. Inside a nested if statement, an *if...elif ... else* inside another *if...elif..else* construct is also possible.

Syntax –
if expression1:
  statement(s)
  if expression2:
    Statement(s)
  elif expression3:
    statement(s)
  else:
    statement(s)
elif expression4:
    statement(s)
else:
    statement(s)

Chapter 4: Learn about Python loops, Strings, Lists, Tuples, and Dictionary

We have already introduced these terms in the previous chapter. Now we will take a look at each one of them in detail so that you can understand their usage in Python programming.

LOOPS

Typically the statements are executed in sequence, but if a situation arises when you are required to execute a block of code many number of times. In Python, a loop statement permits you to execute a statement or a group of statements numerous times. To handle the looping requirement following types of loops are available in Python –

1. **while loop** – this loop repetitively executes a target statement as long as the condition given is true.
   Syntax-
   while expression:
      statement(s)

   Here, it can be a single statement or a block of statements and the condition may be an expression. The loop iterates as long while the condition is true. When the condition becomes false, the program control passes to the line immediately following the loop.

2. **for loop** – these loops have the capability to iterate over items of whichever sequence, like a string or list.
   Syntax-
   for iterating_var in sequence:
      statement(s)

   The sequence which contains an expression is evaluated first and then the first item in a sequence is assigned to the *iterating_var*. After this the statement block is executed. All the items in the list are assigned to *iterating_var*, and the statement(s) block is executed until the entire sequence is exhausted.

3. **Infinite loop–** If a condition never becomes FALSE it becomes an infinite loop. The results in a loop that never ends are called as infinite loops. These loops might be useful in client/server programming where server needs to run continuously for the client programs to communicate with it as and when required.

Using else statements with loops

If an else statement is used with for loop, then the else statement is executed when the loop has exhausted iterating the list. When else is used with a while loop, the else statement is executed when the condition becomes false.

Loop Control Statements

The execution from normal sequence is changed with loop control statements. So when execution leaves a scope, all automatic objects that were created in that scope are destroyed. Listed below are the control statements that are supported by Python –

a) **Break statement** – it ends the current loop statement and transfers execution to the statement immediately following the loop. The break statement can be used in both *for* and *while* loops. Most common use of break statement is when some external condition is triggered requiring a quick exit from loop.
   Syntax-
   break

b) **Continue statement** – The control is returned to the beginning of the while loop. The continue statements reject all the remaining statements in the current iteration of the loop and moves the control back to the top of the loop. It can be used for both *for* and *while* loops.
   Syntax-
   continue

c) **Pass statement** – When a statement is required syntactically but you do not want any command or code to execute, we use pass statement. It is a *null* operation and nothing happens on execution.
   Syntax –
   pass

22

STRINGS

In python, strings can be created by simply enclosing characters in quotes. The single quotes are treated same as double quotes. It is as easy as assigning value to a variable. Python has a built-in string called as 'str' which has many features. A literal in string can expand into multiple lines but there has to be back slash at the end of each line before the new line is created.

Example –
var 1 = 'Goodmorning World!'
var 2 = ' Python Programming'

How to access values in strings?

A character type is not supported by Python, they are considered as strings of length one, therefore also considered as substring. In order to access substring, the square brackets are used for slicing along with the index or indices.

Example –
var 1 = 'Goodmorning World!'
var 2 = "Python Programming"
print "var1[0]:", var1[0]
print "var2[1:5]:", var2[1:5]

result –
var1[0]: G
var2[1:5]: ytho

Updating Strings

Existing strings can be updated by (re)assigning a variable to another string. The new value can be related to a completely different string altogether or to its previous value.

String operators

There are various string operators, assume variable **a** holds 'Hello' and **b** holds 'World'

Operator	Description	Example
*	Repetition –it prints the character twice.	a*2 will give HelloHello
+	Concatenation- adds value on both sides and gives results	a + b will give Hello World
[:]	Range slice – gives characters from given range.	a[1:4] will give ell
[ ]	Slice – gives characters from given index	a[1]will give e
not in	Membership – if a character does not exist in a given string it returns true	M not in a will give 1
in	Membership – if character exists in the given string it returns true	H in a will give 1
r/R	Raw string- it surpasses actual meaning of escape characters	Print r'\n' prints \n and print R'\n' prints \n
%	Format – does string formatting	Read below

<u>String formatting</u>
The string formatting % operator is exclusive to strings and makes up for the bunch of having functions from C's printf family.

Example –
print "My name is %s and weight is %d kg!" % ('Alex', 25)

Result –
My name is Alex and weight is 25kg!

<u>Triple Quotes</u>

A triple quote in Python allows the strings to span in multiple lines which include verbatim TABs, NEWLINEs, and many other special characters. The syntax for triple quotes include three consecutive double or single   quotes.

Changing lower and upper case

In Python, you can change the string to upper case from lower case

str = "this is an example";
print "str.capitalize( ):", str.upper( )

Result –
str.capitalize( ): THIS IS AN EXAMPLE

LISTS

In Python, the fundamental data structure is a sequence. All the elements in a sequence are assigned a number; its index or position. In python, there are six built-in types of sequences and most common are tuples and lists.
Lists are the most flexible data type which can be written as a list of values separated by comma between the square brackets. The items in the list may not be of same type.

Example –
list 1 = ['english', 'french', 1996, 2015];
list2 = [1, 2, 3, 4, 5];
list3 = ["x", "y", "z"]

Just like string indices, list indices also start at 0, and list can be concatenated, sliced and so on.

How to access values in lists?

The square brackets are used for slicing along with the indices or index to get a value at the index.

list 1 = ['english', 'french', 1996, 2015];
list2 = [1, 2, 3, 4, 5, 6, 7];
print "list1[0]:", list1[0]

print "list2[1:5]:", list2[1:5]
Result –

list1[0]: English
list2[1:5]: [2, 3, 4, 5]

Updating Lists

Multiple elements or a single element of lists can be updated by giving the slice on the left-hand side of the assignment operator. It is possible to add elements in a list by using the append( ) method.

Example –

list = ['english', 'french', 1996, 2015];
print "Value available at index 2:"
print list[2]
list[2] = 2016;
print "New value available at index 2:"
print list[2]

Result –

Value available at index 2:
1996
New value available at index 2:
2016

Deleting elements from list

By using either the remove( ) method if you don't know which element to delete or del statement if you know exactly which element(s) you are deleting you can delete a list element.

Example –

list = ['english', 'french', 1996, 2015];

print list1
del list1[2];

print "After deleting value at index 2:"
print list 1

Result-

['english', 'french', 1996, 2015]

After deleting value at index 2:
['english', 'french', 2015]
Similar to Strings, lists also react to * and + operators; they mean repetition and concatenation here as well, except that the outcome is a new list, not a string. As the lists are sequences, slicing and indexing also works in a similar manner as in strings.

Python has some built-in list functions –
1. cmp(list1, list2) – it compares elements in each list
2. max(list) - it returns item from the list with maximum value.
3. len(list) – it gives total strength of the list.
4. min(list)- it returns items from the list with minimum value.
5. List(seq) – it converts tuple into list.

List methods –
1. list.append(obj)- it appends object obj to list
2. list.extend(seq) – it appends the contents of seq to list
3. list.count(obj) – it returns count of how many times obj occurs in list.
4. list.insert(index,obj) – it inserts obj into list at offset index.
5. list.index(obj)- it returns the lowest index in the list that obj appears.
6. list.remove(obj) – it removes object from list
7. list.pop(obj=list[-1])- it removes and returns the last obj from list.
8. list.sort([func]) – sorts objects of list, use compare function if given
9. list.reverse( )- it reverses object of list in place.

TUPLES

The series of unchangeable Python objects are called as tuples. They are sequences similar to lists. Unlike lists, you cannot change tuples and they make use of parentheses, on the other hand square brackets are used in lists. You can create tuples by simply separating values with a comma and optionally these values which are separated by comma can be put inside parentheses.

Example –

tup1 = ('english', 'french', 1996, 2015);
tup2 = (1, 2, 3, 4, 5);
tup3= "x", "y", "z";

Two parentheses consisting of nothing; *tup= ( );* denotes an empty tuple.

In order to write tuple that contains single value a comma needs to be included, even though there is barely a single value; *tup1= (45,);*

How to access values in Tuples?

Make use of the square brackets for slicing, besides the index or indices to get the value available at the index.

Example –
tup1 = ('english', 'french', 1996, 2015);
tup2 = (1, 2, 3, 4, 5, 6, 7);

print "tup1[0]:", tup1[0]
print "tup2[1:5]:", tup2[1:5]

result –

tup1[0]: English
tup2[1:5]: [2, 3, 4, 5]

How to update tuples?

Since tuples are unchangeable you cannot change or update the tuple elements values. You can take parts of existing tuple to make new tuples.

Example –

Tup1 = (14, 32.44);
Tup2 = ('xyz', 'abc');

```
#Below action is not valid for tuples
#tup1[0] =100;
```

```
# Therefore let's create a new tuple
```

```
tup3 = tup1 + tup2;
print tup3
```

result –

(14, 32.44, 'xyz', 'abc')

<u>Deleting elements in tuples</u>

Individual elements of tuples cannot be removed. However, there is nothing wrong in positioning together one more tuple with the undesired elements discarded. In order to completely remove a tuple, just add **del** statement.

Example –

```
tup = ('english', 'french', 1996, 2015);
```

```
print tup
del tup;
print "After deleting tup:"
print tup
```

Result –

('english', 'french', 1996, 2015)

```
After deleting tup:
Traceback (most recent call last):
 file "test.py", line 9, in <module>
   print tup;
NameError: name 'tup' is not defined
```

Please note that an exception is raised because after del tup tuple does not exist.

Similar to strings, tuples react to * and + operators; they denote repetition and concatenation here too, but a new tuple is created as a result and not a string. The indexing and slicing in tuples works in a similar way as it works in strings.

Following are the built-in functions of tuples –

1. cmp(tuple1, tuple2) – it compares the elements in each tuple
2. max(tuple) – it returns item from the tuple with maximum value.
3. len(tuple) – it gives the total length of the tuple.
4. tuple(seq)- it converts a list into a tuple.
5. min(tuple) – it returns item from the tuple with minimum value.

PYTHON DICTIONARY

Dictionary values can be of any kind, but the keys must be of an unchangeable data type such as numbers, strings and tuples.

How to access values in Dictionary?

By using the square brackets along with the key to obtain its value dictionary elements can be accessed.

Example –

dict = {'Name': 'Tom', 'Age': 10, 'Class': 'Fifth'}
print "dict['Name']:", dict['Name']
print "dict['Age']:", dict['Age']

Result –

dict['Name']: Tom
dict['Age']: 10

Properties of Dictionary Keys

a) Per key you cannot have more than one entry, i.e. duplicate key is not allowed. The preceding assignment wins when a duplicate key is encountered.

b) Keys should be unchangeable. By this it means that you may utilize numbers, strings or tuples as dictionary keys but something like ['key'] is not allowed.

Built-in dictionary functions-

1. cmp(dict1,dict2) – compares elements in both
2. str(dict)- produces a printable string
3. len(dict) – gives total length of dictionary
4. type(variable) – returns the type of passed variable.

Built-in dictionary methods-

1. dict.clear( ) – removes all elements of dictionary
2. dict.fromkeys( )- creates a new dictionary with keys from seq and values set to value
3. dic.copy( ) – returns a shallow copy of dictionary
4. dict.get(key, default=None) – returns value or default if key not in dictionary.
5. dict.has_key(key) – returns true if key in dictionary*dict*, otherwise false
6. dict.keys( )- returns list of dictionary dict's keys
7. dict.items( ) – returns a list of *dict's* tuple pairs
8. dict.setfedault(key,default=None) – similar to get, but will set dict[key]= default if *key* is not already in dict.
9. dict.values( )- returns list of dictionary *dict's* values.
10. dict.update( )- adds dictionary *dict2's* key-values pair to *dict*

Chapter 5: Insight into Python Functions, Modules and Classes

FUNCTIONS

A block of code that is organized, reusable, and is used to carry out a single, related action is called as a function. The functions provide better modularity for your application and a high degree of code reusing. Python has many built-in functions but creating your own functions is also possible and these are called as *user-defined* functions.

How to define a Function?

In order to give the necessary functionality you can define a function. Here, are some simple rules for defining a function in Python –

1. A function block begins with the keyword def followed by the function name and parentheses (( )).
2. Any arguments or input parameters must be positioned within these parentheses. Parameters can also be defined within these parentheses.
3. Inside every function the block of code starts with a colon and is indented.
4. The statement return [expression] exits a function, optionally passing back an expression to the caller. The return statement with no arguments is the same as return None.
5. The first statement of a function can be an optional statement; the documentation string of the function or *docstring*.

Syntax –
def functionname (parameters):
  "function_doctsring"
  function_suite
  return [expression]

Parameters, by default have a positional behavior and you need to inform them in the similar order as they were defined.

How to call a function?

By defining a function you only give a name to a function, structures the block of code and specify the parameters that are to be included in the function. Once the basic structure of a function is finalized, you can execute it by calling it from the Python prompt directly or from another function.

Example of function printme( ) is as below –

```
# Function definition is here
def printme(str):
    "This prints a passed string into this function"
    print str
    return;
```

```
# Call the printme function now
printme ("This is first call to user defined function!")
printme ("This is second call to the same function")
```

Output –
This is first call to user defined function!
This is second call to the same function

In Python, all parameters (arguments) are passed by reference. This means what a parameter refers to inside a function, if you change it, the change gets reflected back in the calling function.

Function Arguments

By using following types of arguments you can call a function –
   a) Required arguments –these are the arguments passed to a function in correct positional order. In this the number of arguments in the function call should exactly match with the function definition.
   b) Keyword arguments – These are related to function calls. Once keyword argument is used in a function call, the parameter name identifies the arguments to the caller. This allows for skipping of arguments or places them out of order since the keywords given to match the values with parameters is used by the Python interpreter.
   c) Default arguments –in the function call if a value is not provided for the argument this argument assumes a default value.
   d) Variable-length arguments – While defining a function it may be required to process a function for additional arguments than specified, these are

called as variable-length arguments. Unlike default and required arguments, they are not named in the function definition. The variable name that carries the value of all non-keyword variable arguments an asterisk is placed before it. Tuple will remain empty in case there are no extra arguments specified during a function call.

Scope of Variables

In a program, all variables may not be accessible at all locations. This depends on where you have declared a variable. The portion of the program where you can access a particular identifier is determined by the scope of variables. There are two basic scopes –
   a) Global – Variables that are defined outside the function body have a global scope. These can be accessed throughout the program body by all functions.
   b) Local – Variables that are defined inside the function body have a local scope. These can be accessed only inside a function in which they are declared.

MODULES

Modules help in organizing the code logically. The code becomes easy to use and understand by grouping the related code into module. A Python object with arbitrarily named attributes that can bind and reference is called module. In simple words, module is a file that consists of Python code. It can define variables, functions, and classes.

Example of simple module support.py -

```
def print_func( par ):
    print " Hi:", par
    return
```

Import Statememt

Any Python source file can be used as a module by executing an import statement in some other Python source file.

Syntax –

import module1[, module2[,. . .moduleN]

From import statement

Specific attributes can be imported from a module into the current namespace with the help of *from import* statements**.**

Syntax –
from modname import name1[, name2[,. . .nameN]]

From...import * statement

The *from..import*statement* makes the import of all names possible from a module into the current namespace.

from modname import*

Locating Modules
The module is searched by the Python interpreter in the below mentioned sequence when a module is imported.
  a) Current directory
  b) In case the module isn't found, the Python looks into every directory in the shell variable PYTHONPATH
  c) The default path is checked in Python, if else fails.

The module search path is stored in the system module sys as the **sys.path**variable. This variable contains the current directory, PYTHONPATH, and the installation dependent default.
PYTHONPATH – it is an environment variable, which consists of a list of directories.
Syntax-
For windows -
set PYTHONPATH=c:\python20\lib;

For UNIX-
set PYTHONPATH=/usr/local/lib/python

Namespaces and scoping

A namespace is a dictionary of variable names (keys) and their corresponding objects (values)

Variable can be accessed in Python in both local and global namespace. In case a global and local variable has the same name, the global variable is overshadowed by the local variable. All functions have their own local namespace. The same scoping rules are followed by classes as ordinary functions. Whether variables are global or local is a informed guess made by Python. An assumption is made that any variable is local which has been assigned a value in a function. Therefore, for assigning a value to a global variable inside a function, the global statement needs to be used first. The statement *global VarName*tells that VarName is global. Searching the local namespace for the variable is stopped by Python.

The dir( ) function-

It returns a systematic list of strings consisting of the names defined by a module. List consists of all the functions, modules and variables that are defined in a module.

The globals( ) and locals( ) functions-

These functions can be used to return names in the local and local namespaces depending on the location from where they are called. If from inside a function a globals( ) is called, it will return all the names that can be globally accessed from that function. In case locals( ) is called from inside a function, it will return names that can be locally accessed from that function. The return type for both the functions is dictionary. So the names can be extracted using the keys( ) function.

The reload( ) function

The code in the top level portion of a module is executed only once when the module is imported into a script. However, if you want to execute the top level code again, then use the reload( ) function. A previously imported module is imported again by this function.

Syntax –

reload(module_name)

In syntax, *module_name* is the name of the module to be reloaded and not the string consisting of the module name.

CLASSES

As we know that Python is an object-oriented language, therefore using and creating objects and classes is easy. A class is a user-defined model for an object that defines a set of attributes that portray any object of the class. The attributes are the data members and methods, associated via dot notation. Data member is an instance variable or a class variable that holds data related with a class and its objects. The instance variable is a variable that is defined inside a method and belongs to the current instance of a class.

How to create classes?

A new class definition is created by a *class* statement. The name of the class straight away follows the keyword *class* followed by a colon.

class ClassName:
    'Optional class documentation string'
    class_suite
- A class has a documentation string, which can be accessed via ClassName._doc_.
- Each component statement that defines class members, functions and data attributes exist in the *class_suite*.

How to create instances of class?

Use class name to call the class and pass in no matter what arguments its *_init_* method accepts for creating an instance of a class.

How to access attributes?

Dot operator with object need to be used in order to access the object's attributes.

Built-in class attributes

Dot operator can be used to access the built-in attributes–

a) _dict_ - dictionary containing class's namespace
b) _name_ - class name
c) _doc_ - class documentation string or none, if undefined.
d) _bases_ - probably a vacant tuple containing the base classes in the order of their occurrence in the base class list.
e) _module_ - the module name in which class is defined. This attribute in interactive mode is "_main_".

Garbage Collection

In Python, to make the memory space free, objects (class instances or built-in) that are not required are deleted automatically. Garbage collection is a method by which Python from time to time recovers memory blocks that are no longer in use. Python's garbage collector runs while the program is being executed and is triggered when an object's reference count reaches zero. An object's reference count increases when it is positioned in a container (tuple, list or dictionary) or is assigned a new name. The object's reference count decreases when it is deleted with *del*, its reference goes out of scope or it is reassigned. Python automatically collects when an object's reference count reaches zero.

Class inheritance

A pre-existing class can be used for deriving and creating a new class instead of begining from scratch by listing the parent class after the new class name inside parentheses. The attributes of its parent class are inherited by the child class, and these attributes can be used as if they were defined in the child class. Just like their parent class the derived classes can be declared. Though, after the class name a list of base classes to inherit from is given.

Syntax –

class SubClassName (ParentClass1[, ParentClass2,. . .]):
    'Optional class documentation string'
    class_suite (Python - Environment Setup)

Chapter 6: Exception handling

<u>Exception</u>

An event that interrupts the standard flow of the program's instructions at the time of execution is called as an exception. Typically, when such a situation is encountered by a Python script that it cannot handle, it raises an exception. In other words, an exception is a Python object that depicts an error. When an exception is raised in Python script, it either the exception is handled immediately or it is terminated.

<u>How to handle an exception?</u>

In case you find a suspicious code in a program, then the program can be defended by putting that code in a **try:** block. After this include an **except:**statement followed by a block of code which manages the problem as gracefully as possible.

Syntax –

```
try:
   You do your operations here;
   ......................................
except Exception I:
   If there is Exception I, then execute this block.
Except Exception II:
   If there is Exception II, then execute this block.
   ......................................
else:
   If there is no exception then execute this block.
```

Please note –
- A single try statement can have multiple except statements.
- A generic except clause can also be provided, which manages any exception.
- An else-clause can also be included after except clause(s). If the code in try: block does not raise an exception the code in the else-block is executed.

- A better place for code that does not need the try: block's protection is the else-block.

Except Clause with no exception –all the exceptions that occur are caught by the try-except statement. However, it doesn't make the programmer recognize the root cause of the problem that may occur.

Except clause with multiple exceptions- the same except statement to handle multiple exceptions can be used.

Try-finally clause – The finally: block with try: block can be used. In the finally block you can place any code that must execute, irrespective of the fact that the try-block has raised an exception or not.

Argument of an exception – An argument is a value that gives more information about the problem and an exception can have an argument. You can catch an exception's argument by providing a variable in the except clause.

Raising Exceptions

You can raise exceptions in several ways by using the raise statement.

Syntax –

raise [Exception [, args [, traceback]]]

Here, *argument* is a value for the exception argument and *Exception* is the type of exception. However, argument is optional; if not supplied, the exception argument is None. For example, an exception can be a class, string or an object. Most exceptions that Python core raises are classes, with an argument that is an instance of the class.

In Python, you are allowed to create your own exceptions by deriving classes from the standard built-in exceptions. (Python Exceptions Handeling)

Conclusion

This brings us to the end of this edition of the book. We can easily say that Python is a powerful language and that is the reason why all big companies are looking for programmers who have the knowledge of this dynamic language.

Before we end, let's summarize on what we have learned so far. The book began with basic introduction to Python, its features, how to install and set up. We also understood that Python has fewer syntactical constructs thus making it easy and readable. All Python fundamentals i.e. variables, data types, operators, lists, strings, loops, tuples and dictionary have been covered in the book.

We have also ensured that the concept of function, classes, and modules is covered for a better understanding of the language. The last section on exception handling can be useful in practical application.

To conclude, we can say that once you are clear on the basics of Python you will be able to create almost anything you want.

Thank you once again for downloading this book, hope it has given you a meaningful insightinto Python.

Works Cited

Python - Environment Setup. n.d. 2017.
    <https://www.tutorialspoint.com/python/python_environment.htm>.

Python Exceptions Handeling. n.d. 2017.
    <https://www.tutorialspoint.com/python/python_exceptions.htm>.

Book 2

Hacking

By: PG WIZARD BOOKS

Top Online Handbook in Exploitation of Computer Hacking, Security, and Penetration Testing!

Hacking: Top Online Handbook in Exploitation of Computer Hacking, Security, and Penetration Testing!

Table of Contents

Hacking: Top Online Handbook in Exploitation of Computer Hacking, Security, and Penetration Testing!

Introduction

The world of hacking is an interesting world. Most of us only understand what is going on based on the movies that we watch or the news that we read about hackers stealing identities of those around them. These are parts of the whole hacking world, but there is so much more that comes with it. For example, some hackers are considered ethical hackers, which means that they are going to work to prevent others from getting onto their own systems, or the systems of others they are working for.

This guidebook is going to take some time to discuss the basics of the hacking world. We will start out with the difference between white hat hackers and black hat hackers and how each of them are going to work on the hacks that they are creating. We will then move on to working with how to map out your hack, especially if you want to check for vulnerabilities inside of your own system. And then the rest of the book will spend time looking at some of the common types of hacking that you can do including man in the middle hacks and even hacking passwords.

Even when it comes to hacking into a network that you are allowed to be on, it is important to learn how to do some basic hacks because you will be using the same methods that the black hat hackers are doing as well. This guidebook is going to help you to get started with doing some of the hacks that you need to ensure that you are getting the best results that you want.

Chapter 1: Some of the Basics of Computer Hacking

The process of hacking has gotten a bad name, mainly because of all the stories that have gone on in the media and in the movies about this topic. We may imagine someone who is just trying to get onto a system the are not allowed to be in or about someone who hacks into the government computers in order to get some important information and save the day. But there are many different facets that come up when we are talking about hacking and while some hackers are interested in stealing information and being places they aren't allowed to be, there are some who are more interested in learning hacking in order to protect their own computer systems and information.

There are two main types of computer hacking that you can come across. These include:

- Black hat hacking: this is the type that is found inside the movies. This is when someone tries to get onto a system that they don't belong, without the permission of the person who owns the system. Often this is done so that the hacker is able to get information they are not supposed to have, such as your personal information and credit card numbers.
- White hat hacking: this is the type of hacking that you may do when trying to keep your computer system and information safe from someone who may try to get the information and use it for their own reasons. Also, white hat hackers may also work with a big company, working on hacking on the system to see if it is vulnerable, in order to keep other people out of the system.

Both of these types of hackers are going to use the same methods to do the hacking, but the reasons behind the hacking are going to be completely different. It is important to note that black hat hacking is illegal and if you do this kind of hacking, it could end up with you going to jail and in a lot of trouble. But there is nothing wrong with hacking on to a system that you have permission to be on, such as your own personal computer, to help keep it safe or as part of your job.

Hacking: Top Online Handbook in Exploitation of Computer Hacking, Security, and Penetration Testing!

Penetration testing

Now that we have a little basics of the world of hacking, it is time to look more into the world of computer hacking. We will start this out with penetration testing. This is known as an authorized attempt in order to exploit a computer system in the hopes of learning the flaws that are inside of it so that you can work to make it more secure. When you are given the assignment to do a penetration test, or you decide to do it on your own system, you will be investigating the system in order to prove that there are vulnerabilities in the network.

After you are done with doing the penetration test, the mitigation measures will be made in order to address any of the issues that you found and fix the issues that you discovered during this test. It is basically a process of finding the threats that are present inside of the system and then come up with a good plan that is going to take care of the issues that show up during the test. Doing these on occasion to the system can ensure that you catch the vulnerabilities inside the system before someone else gets on and steals your information.

Penetration testing is also known as ethical hacking. There is a very thin line that is present between vulnerability assessment and penetration testing. These terms are often interchanged but they are not really the same thing. For example, the vulnerability assessment is going to be responsible for evaluations the system for any security issues that may be present already. But the penetration test is going to be the test that is used in order to exploit and also proves that these security issues exist. The test is going to allow the hacker to test out the system as an outside source so that they can see how the vulnerabilities are affecting things.

As a white hat hacker, you would want to go through the system and perform the same actions that a black hat hacker would do on the system in this kind of test. You would try to get onto the system to see how bad the vulnerabilities are and to determine what information others are able to see. While the black hat hacker would simply do this in the hopes of trying to get onto the system and exploit it for their own personal gains, you are going to find out where these things are and learn how to close them up. Even though both of you will use the same methods in order to get onto the system, you are going to have different reasons for getting onto the system.

A hacking lab

As a beginner to working on hacking, you may want to consider working in a hacking lab. This is a safe environment that you are able to work in with the attacks and the traffic to see how they respond to different things that you are working on, without them getting out of hand and heading to places they are not supposed to be. This is a good place for a beginner to get started with because it allows you to get some practice without ruining anything in the system or causing some issues. Once you get a little bit more of the practice into the thing, you will be able to move out of the hacking lab and have some fun with hacking, and do some of the tests, on a real network.

While there are some differences in the reason for hacking between a white hat and a black hat hacker, both of these groups are going to use the same kinds of skills and techniques in order to get the information that they want. The trick here is for the white hat hacker to know just as much, of not more, and to be faster at finding the vulnerabilities compared to the black hat hacker. This will help to keep the system protected and ensures that the other group isn't able to get information they are not supposed to have.

Chapter 2: Mapping Out the Hack Before Beginning

So before we get too far in this process, it is important to come up with the plan that you want to use. This is meant to give you a good idea of what you need to do and where you want to look for some of these vulnerabilities inside of your system. The strategies that you will use are important, but you really need to focus on having a good plan in place before you get too far in this process.

When you are trying to find some of the vulnerabilities that are needed, you don't need to waste your time checking all of the protocols for security at the same time. This can make it a bit confusing and sometimes it is going to make you deal with more problems than you want because too much information is coming towards you. This means that you should break your system up into parts and then test each of these parts so that the work is more manageable overall.

For the most part, it is a good idea to start out with the application or system that you are worried about the most, and then go down the list until you get to each of them. To help you to determine which of the systems you should work with first, consider these questions:

- If the system is attacked, which system or application is going to cause the most issues. Which one has the most information or would be the hardest to fix up if it were lost.
- If the system is attacked, which application is going to be the easiest for the hacker to get in to.
- Which sections of the system are you working on and are considered the least documented, which means that they are rarely checked. Do you notice some that you have never seen there before?

As you answer these questions, it is going to become easier to figure out which applications you should work on first and it is easier to go through the whole process and find the results that you want. There are many places that you are able to check out to make sure the tests are run the proper way including the routers and the switches, workstations and laptops, operating systems, databases and applications, firewalls, files, and emails servers and more. It is possible that you will need to run many tests to get all of these so take your time and try them out to see where the vulnerabilities may lie.

When should I do my hack?

Once you have a good list of the applications and devices that you want to check, the next question that you may have is when is a good time to hack. You will need to make sure that you complete the hacks during a time that is going to cause the least amount of disruption in the company or on your own personal computer. This means during the peak hours of the day, you should not be doing these hacks because they could potentially cause a lot of slow down and issues with the system and depending on the type of hack that you do, and if it goes well or not, it could even shut down the network when it is needed most. The best time to complete the tasks is when there is going to be minimal disruption, so coming in after hours is often best since few people will be on the system or the building could be closed and no one will even notice.

The time that works the best for these hacks will vary depending on the situation. For example, if you are doing one of these hacks on your own computer, the timing may not matter as much because you would just pick a time when you are free to do the hacks and call it good. On the other hand, if you are doing this as a job for your employer, you will need to abide by their busy times and pick one that is not going to interfere with the business, especially if the hack does cause some issues.

Will others see what I am doing?

When you are working on these hacks in order to find some of the vulnerabilities that are in the system, you need to think just like a criminal hacker would, since these are the type of people that would try to get onto the system. Sometimes being able to look at the system through fresh eyes can make all the difference. For example, when you are used to using this system, you are an insider and could have troubles seeing what is going on in the system, but it is important that you make sure that when you do the hacks, no one else is able to see what you are doing. The criminal hacker would be careful about who is able to notice their presence so you would want to be the same way.

Hacking: Top Online Handbook in Exploitation of Computer Hacking, Security, and Penetration Testing!

Now, it is your job to also check out what the hacker is able to see on your system. Hackers are always trying to find out as much information about the system as possible to make it easier to get onto it, and there are trails left all over the place for them to look at. As the ethical hacker of the system, it is your responsibility to find out what kind of information is out there for the other hackers to find and then learn how to diminish these trails to make your website and system harder to mess with. There are several different scanner types that you are able to use, such as a port scanner, so that you can see what information that is being shared, making it easier to catch some of these issues. Some of the other searches that you can do to protect your network includes doing a search online for the following information:

Any contact details. This is going to be information that can point back to the people connected with your business. Some options like USSearch and ChoicePoint are good ones to visit and see if your information is present there.

Look for any recent press releases that may talk about changes that have happened in the organization.

Look through any of the acquisitions and mergers of the company.

Always see if you can find any SEC documents about the company online.

Any patents or trademarks that are associated with this company.

Incorporation filings. These are also found through the SEC, but sometimes they are located elsewhere.

Be as thorough as possible about this point so that you have a good idea of what hackers are able to find out about your company or about your network. Often doing a keyword search is not going to bring up the results that you would like so you need to work with some advanced searches to find out all the information that you would like. At this point, you have a good idea of the different things that your computer or your network is sending out to other people and you can create the plan to get it all under control. Deleting information from online can help but running some port and network scans are great as well. Go through as many of these scans and tests as you can to help keep the computer network as safe as possible.

Chapter 3: Doing a Spoofing Attack

The first type of attack that we are going to explore is the spoofing attack. Whether you are working as a criminal hacker or as an ethical hacker, there are a lot of things that you can work with in order to get into a system that you shouldn't be on. As a hacker, you are responsible for researching and having some patience to wait in order to find the vulnerability that is on the system or network before taking the next move. But with the right kind of work, it is easier to get on the network and often a few different options are going to show up for you. One method that you can use is the spoofing technique that allows you to convince the computer system that you should be there so that you can get all the information that you want. Let's take a look at how this works and how you can make it happen with your hacking.

Spoofing

One of the first techniques that we are going to explore in this guidebook is spoofing. This is basically going to be a technique where the hacker is able to pretend that they are another person, software, website, or organization in order to convince the network that they are supposed to be here. The hacker is meant to look like this other person so that the network will allow them through the security protocols and then the hacker can get through where they want, get the information that is needed, and even leave the system before anyone else is able to see them. There are a few options that you are able to pick from when it comes to the spoofing technique including:

IP spoofing

With the technique of IP spoofing, the hacker is going to mask up their IP address or make changes to it so that the network things that the hacker belongs to the network. The hacker is able to make these changes so that the IP address either matches up with what is allowed on the network or it is one that the network is going to be familiar with. With this method, the hacker is able to be in any part of the world that they want, but the network is still going to allow them to get on because the IP address matches up in some manner. Once the hacker is able to get on to the system, they have the ability to take over this network, change files, delete things, and do some other tasks without ever being detected.

If the hacker is able to pull off this technique, it is very successful because it has convinced the network that the hacker is supposed to be there. The trusted IP address is found by the hacker and then it is used to get onto the network and make the changes that are needed. The hacker will be able to use this in order to gain full access to the whole system, whether they choose to sit around and wait for a good opportunity or they choose to do an attack and get the information they want right away.

DNS spoofing

Another spoofing technique is known as DNS spoofing. This method is going to trick a user who is trying to get onto a legitimate site. The hacker will take the IP address and then when a user clicks on it, they will be sent to a malicious website where the hacker has complete control. Sometimes the hacker will take over a legitimate website and turn it to their use, but often they will change around a letter or two to trick people. Users who aren't paying attention or who type in the address wrong will be sent to a bad website and the hacker can take credentials and private information from the user.

Often the user will not realize that they are being tricked. They will get onto the website and figure that it is just where they want to be. They can put in private information, send payment, and more while the hacker is collecting it all privately.

For the hacker to get this to work, they need to have the same LAN as their target. This requires the hacker to search for a weak password on one of the machines that is on the network, something that is possibly even from a different location. Once the hacker accomplishes this, they will be able to redirect all users to their website and easily monitor the activities that are done there.

Email spoofing

Email spoofing is one of the most common types of spoofing, which is one of the reasons that people should be very careful about the emails that they are receiving, sending, and clicking on. This can be a useful technique when the hacker wants to try and get past some of the security that is placed on email accounts. Most email servers are going to be good at recognizing if someone looks like they are legitimate and when something is spam, but there are also times when the hacker will be able to get past this and can send malicious attachments.

The most common form of this is when the hacker is able to pretend to be someone else inside the system so that they can intercept the emails from both parties, either read them or make changes, and then send the emails on without either of the two parties knowing. This can be really useful to the hacker because they can really get stuff done, and get ahold of private information that might be hidden elsewhere.

Phone number spoofing

When it comes to using phone number spoofing, the hacker is going to get ahold of some false numbers, or even area codes, so that they can mask their location. This is the best way for the hacker to be able to get into some of the voicemail messages that you have, and even to send out some text messages using this number. The target is often misled about where the hacker is from. Often this one is used when the hacker wants to pretend that they belong to a government office to trick the target.

The spoofing attacks can be difficult because often the network administrator is not even able to find out these attacks. The hacker will be able to stay on the network and cause almost as much damage as they want to these systems, without ever being found. It is often only after the hacker causes a big mess or when important information is leaked out that the hacker is finally caught and taken off the system. The hacker will be able to use just these kinds of hacks or some of the others in order to get the results they want and often they will be undetected by others on the same network.

Chapter 4: Man in the Middle Attacks

In addition to being able to do the spoofing attacks that we talked about in the previous chapter, it is also possible for a hacker to do a man in the middle attack. Sometimes the hacker will do this as a passive attack in order to just get on the system and see what information they are able to get, and other times they will use an active attack to get information, slow down the system, or cause some other form of problems.

When it comes to the man in the middle attacks, the hacker is able to do this with a form of spoofing that is called Address Resolution Protocol, or ARP. With this, the hacker is able to send messages that are false, but which are going to look normal, all over the network that they are working on. When it is pulled off, these fake messages allow the hacker to link up with another IP address of one of the users on the network. Once the hacker is done with this part, they can receive any of the data that all of the users are sending with this IP address and use it in the way that they would like.

So basically with this, the hacker is taking over an IP address and making it their own. They will receive all files, communication, and other information that is meant to go to the original user and they can use it however they would like. The hacker has the ability to get onto the network while receiving all traffic that goes on the network as well.

1. Session hijacking—this is when the hacker will use their false ARP to still the user's ID for the session. The hacker will be able to hold on to the information about the traffic and use it at a later date to get access to the account.

2. Denial of service attack—this is an attack done when the ARP spoof links several IP addresses to the target. During this attack, the data that should be sent to the other IP addresses are sent to one device. This is going to result in an overload of data.

3. Man in the middle attack—with this attack, the hacker is going to pretend that they are non-existent inside the network. Since they are hidden, they are able to modify and intercept messages that are sent between two or more users on the network. The one network may send a legitimate email, but the hacker will take it and change the information to be more

malicious before sending it on. The second user will open the malicious information, believing it to be safe.

Now that we know a bit more about a man in the middle attack, you are probably interested in learning some of the steps that are needed in order to complete the man in the middle attack. Here are some of the options that you can use and we are going to bring in the tool called Backtrack in order to get this done:

Do the research

The first step that you will need to do is find out the data that is needed to begin. The tool Wireshark is a good one to work with because it will help you to get all of this information to get on to the system. Firing up this tool on the network is going to allow the hacker to see what traffic is able to get onto the network through either the wireless or wired networks and is a really good place to get started for an access point.

Use your wireless adapter in monitor mode

Now that we have done some research, it is time to work with the wireless adapter and change it over to what is known as the monitor mode. This mode is going to make it easier for you to see the traffic that goes into your connection, even the traffic that isn't allowed to be there. This method is the one that you will work when using hubbed networks because you will find that the hubbed ones won't have as much security as you will find with the switched networks.

If you are able to see what information is going between the users that are on the switch, or you would like to make a bypass over this completely, you are able to work on making changes to the entries that are inside of your CAM table that is responsible for mapping out the IP and MAC addresses that are sending information to each other. When you are able to make changes to these entries, it is easier to get ahold of this traffic, make changes or at least read through it, and then send it back on without others knowing. The ARP spoofing attack is going to make this easier to accomplish.

Turning on backtrack

Now that you have changed the adapter and gotten it set up the way that you would like, it is time to fire up the Backtrack that you would like to use. You will need to pull up the Backtrack and then pull up all three terminals. Next, you will replace the MAC address from the target client with your personal MAC address. The code for doing this is: arpspoof [client IP] [server IP].

Once you do that, you will need to reverse the order of the IP addresses in the string that you just used. This is going to tell the server that your computer is the authorized one so that you are allowed to get onto the system and perform other tasks. You are basically going to become the server and the client so you can

57

receive packets of information and change them how you wish. It also goes the other way around.

For those who are using Linux, you can use the built in feature known as ip_forward, which will make it easier to forward the packets you are receiving. Once you turn this feature on, you will be able to go back into Backtrack and forward these packets with the commandecho 1 >/proc/sys/net/ipv4/ip_forward.

This command is going to make it easier to be right between the client and the server. You will get all the information that goes between these two and as the hacker, you can use the information as you wish. You could look at the system, take personal information, or change anything you want about information that is shared.

Check out your traffic

At this point, you should be able to get access to all of the information that the users are all sending through the network. You will get to be right in the front row of this action and you can either watch the information that is being sent or grab ahold of some of it and make changes before sending it all back through the system again. You can use your BackTrack tool in order to sniff out the traffic and get a nice clear picture of the system. You need to take some time to activate this feature in order to make it work, but it can make things easier to work with.

Get your data as well as the credentials

Now you will just need to wait around and see when the client is logging into the server. Once the client logs on, you will be able to see their username and password coming up right in front of you. This means that the information is going to be right in front of you, making it easier to record and use it whenever you would like. Since the users and the administrators are all going to use these same credentials on all of the systems on the computer, you can keep using these credentials in order to get anywhere that you would like. You are now right in the middle of all the information on the system and you can use it in any manner that you would like, without other users on the system having any idea.

And now you are done creating your very first man in the middle attack. This is a great way for you to get in the middle of the all the action on a system, and the other users will have no idea that you are there. There are many things that you are able to do from here, such as intercepting information, changing the messages that are sent, slowing down the system, and even getting ahold of some classified information. this can really put the hacker right in the middle of the action so it is a great way for you to get started.

Hacking: Top Online Handbook in Exploitation of Computer Hacking, Security, and Penetration Testing!

Chapter 5: How to Use Hacking to Get Passwords

The biggest target of hackers is to get passwords, mainly because they are really easy to get. Most people think that they just need to come up with a longer password in order to protect themselves, but there is more to it than that. If the hacker is able to use some of the tricks we stated earlier in this chapter, it does not matter how long your username and password is, they will still have it sent directly to them.

Confidential log in information, including passwords, are considered the weakest links in security because the only thing it relies on is secrecy. Once the secret is out, the security is pretty much gone. This is why it is such a big deal when a big company is hacked and all the username and passwords are leaked. The hacker is now able to get onto the system and use your information however they wish. Sometimes, the user themselves will inadvertently give out their own password for hackers to use.

So how do you hack a password? There are several ways that the hacker can do this including a physical attack, social engineering, and inference. There are also a few different tools that are used to crack passwords including:

1. Cain and Abel—this one is good to help with Windows RDP passwords, Cisco IOS hashes and more.

2. Elmcomsoft Distributed Password Recovery—this one is able to get PGP and Microsoft Office passwords and has been used in order to crack distributed passwords as well as recover up to 10,000 networked computers.

3. Elmcomsoft System Recovery—this has the ability to set administrative credentials, rest expirations on passwords, and reset passwords on Windows computers.

4. Ophcrack—this will use rainbow tables to crack passwords for Windows.

5. Pandora—this can be a good one to use to crack Novell Netware accounts either online or offline.

Some of these tools do have a shortfall because they will require the hacker to have physical access to the system they are hacking. But once the hacker has access to the system that you are protecting, they will be able to dig into all of your encrypted and password protected files with just a few tools.

Hacking: Top Online Handbook in Exploitation of Computer Hacking, Security, and Penetration Testing!

Often, the hacker is not going to have access to your computer to do a password hack and they will rely on some other tools. Some examples of other methods used to hack a password include:

1. Dictionary attacks—these are attacks that will make use of dictionary words against the password database. This makes it easier to figure out if there is a weak password in the system.

2. Brute force attacks—these are capable of cracking all types of passwords because they are going to use all combinations of numbers, special characters, and letters until the device is cracked. The biggest flaw with this technique is that it can take a ton of time to uncover the password.

3. Rainbow attacks—these are good for cracking any hashed passwords. The tool is really fast compared to others, but it is not able to uncover passwords that are more than 14 characters.

4. Keystroke logging—this is one of the best techniques for cracking a password because it is asking the targeted computer to basically send over the information. The hacker is able to place a recording device on the targeted system to take in all the keystrokes done on the computer. The information is then sent over using programs such as KeyGhost.

5. Searching for weak storages—there are a lot of applications in computers that will store the passwords locally, making them vulnerable to a hacker. When you have physical access to the computer, it is easy to find the passwords through text searches and sometimes they are even stored on the application.

6. Grab the passwords remotely—often it is not possible to physically access a system, it is still possible to get the passwords from a remote location. You will need to do a spoofing attack first, exploit the SAM file and have the information sent to you.

Once the hacker has access to these passwords, it is easier for them to get the information that they want. They can use the passwords to get onto the network, to get to emails, find out financial accounts, and so much more. You must remember that passwords are a huge vulnerability in your system and to figure out more secure ways to protect your system.

Chapter 6: Getting Through Internet Connections for the Hack

If you would like to work on hacking online, you will need to learn how to get through the internet connection, as well as the security features, that are found online. Here we are going to talk about how to hack through a WEP connection as well as how to perform an evil twin hack so that you can check to see if your system is susceptible to this kind of attack or not:

How to hack a WEP connections

While there are a few different types of internet connections that you can work with in order to hack, this is one of the easiest to go through. If this is the one that your system is working with, you will definitely need to run through a few tests to see if you have been hacked or if you can make it more secure. Some of the things that you will need to check and hack through a WEP connection includes:

1. To get started, load up the BackTrack and the aircrack-ng. you can fire up BackTrack and then make sure that it is plugged into the wireless adapter to see if it is running. You can type in lwconfi in order to see if this is working. The program is then going to tell you which of the adapter it can recognize and if this is working properly, it is going to see yours.
2. Then take the wireless adapter and set it so it is at promiscuous mode. This will allow you to see what other connections are available and you can type in "airmon-ng start wlano" in order to do this. You can then change the name of your interface to have it read momo. You now have the adapter inside of monitor mode and you can type in "airodump-ng mono" to see which access points are available and what is attached to them.
3. Start capturing your access point. You will need to pick which connection you want to get on and then capture it. You can do this by using the command

   a. Airodump-ng –bssid [BSSID of target] -c [channel number] -w WEPcrack momo.

   b. Once you enter this command, the BackTrack is going to start capturing packets fro the access point on the right channel. This will

> send the hacker all the packets that it needs in order to decode any passkeys that are present so they can get onto the wireless. However, it is important to realize that getting these packets will often take some time. If you need to get the packets quickly, it may be time to add in an ARP traffic.

4. Inject the ARP traffic—for anyone who doesn't want to wait around for the packets from WEPkey capture, doing an ARP packet and having it replay can help you get the packets that you need to crack the WEPkey. Since you already have the MAC and BSSID address from the target thanks to doing step 3, you will be able to use them to enter the following command:

   a. Aireplay-ng -3 -b [BSSID] – [MAC address] mon0

   b. This will allow you to capture the ARPs through the access point of the target. You must keep going in order to capture the IVs that will come in as well.

5. Crack the WEPkey. Once you have the necessary amount of IVs in your WEPcrack file, it is time to run your aircrack-ng. Put in the command:

   a. Aircrack-ng [name of file]

   b. The aircrack-ng will enter the passkey in a hexadecimal format. You will just need to apply this key into your remote access point and then you are on the program. You can use it for free internet, to take over a computer on the system, and much more.

The Evil Twin Hack

The evil twin hack is an access point that will act like the access point that a user connects to, but it is manipulative. The target will just see their regular access point and think it is safe to get on, but this manipulative access point is used by a hacker to send the target to the hackers' premade access point, where the hacker can then start a dangerous man in the middle attack.

As a beginner hacker, you may need some practice doing the evil twin attack. Some basic steps to try out include:

1. Turn on BackTrack and start the program airmon-ng. Check to see if your wireless card is running properly by entering bt>iwconfig.

2. Once you have the wireless card, it is time to put it into monitor mode. You will be able to do this by entering the command bt >airmon-ng start wlan0.

3. Now you need to fire up the airdump-ng. you will start capturing the wireless traffic that your wireless card is able to detect. To do this, enter

the command bt >airodump-ng mono. After this step, you will have the ability to see all access points that are in range and can pick out the one that belongs to your target.

4. You will need to wait for when the target connects. Once the target gets onto the access point, you can copy the BSSID and the MAC address that you want to hack into.

5. Now the hacker will need to create an access point that has the same credentials.

    a. First, pull up a new terminal and type in bt > airbase-ng -a [BSSID] –essid ["SSID of target] -c [channel number] mono

    b. This is going to create the access point that you want. It will look the same as the original access point so the target will click on it, but it puts the hacker right in the middle as the one in control.

6. De-authenticate the target—for the target to get onto your new access point, you will need to get them off the one they are connected to. Since many wireless connections will go with 802.11, everyone who is connected to the access point will be de-authenticated when you do this. When the target tries to get back on to the internet, they will connect automatically to the one with the strongest signal, which in this case will be your manipulated access point.

    a. To get the target off their access point, make sure to do the following command: bt > aireplay-ng –deauth 0 -a [BSSID of target]

7. Turn the signal of the evil twin up. The trick on this one is to get the fake access point to have a strong signal. It needs to be at least as strong, but preferably stronger, than the original point of access. This can be tricky because you are likely further away than the original access point.

    a. Iwconfig wlano txpower 27 will help you to turn up the signal on your access point.

    b. This can add 500 milliwatts to your power. If you are too far away though, this may not be enough. You either need to be closer to the target or consider a newer wireless card that is able to go up to 2000 milliwatts.

8. Put the evil twin to good use—once you have established the evil twin and you know that the target and the network are all connected to it, it is time to take the steps needed in order to detect all the activities going on in the system. It often depends on what you want to do with the system for where you will go from here.

Hacking: Top Online Handbook in Exploitation of Computer Hacking, Security, and Penetration Testing!

    a. There are a lot of options of what to do at this point. Hackers who have gone and created an evil twin are interested in more than just free wireless so they will often do man in the middle attacks, intercept traffic, add in new traffic, or steal information from the system, often without the target realizing.

Conclusion

Working in the world of hacking can be really interesting. There are a lot of people who are interested in knowing how to protect their own systems from a hacker getting on and finding out information that they shouldn't, but most of us assume that going through the process of hacking is going to be too difficult to get started. But with the help of this guidebook, we are going to be able to learn some of the basics of working in hacking and how to protect your own network easily.

Inside this guidebook, we spent some time talking about the different ways that you are able to work with hacking. We started with some of the basics of hacking, such as the differences between white hat hackers and the black hat hackers and discussed how they often use some of the same methods to get things done. In addition, we talked about working on mapping your attack so that you have a plan and how to work with spoofing, man in the middle attacks, password hacks, and even how to hack through different connections online. All of these can come together to help you understand how to do a good hack and keep things safe from a hacker.

It is important that you learn how to keep your information safe from others who will try to get on your network and steal it. This guidebook is going to teach you some more about hacking and how you can use it for your needs and to keep your computer system safe.